More Praise for Hal Sirowitz:

"The portrait of the mother in [*Mother Said*] is as affecting in its way as the portrait of Portnoy's mother in *Portnoy's Complaint*."
—*Boston Sunday Globe*

"I like to think of him as the Kafka of Flushing, Queens. . . .With a comic's dead-on, deadpan delivery he spins out heartbreaking and hilarious poems that are wise and devastating at the same time."
—Catherine Bowman, *Word Of Mouth*, poems featured on
NPR's *All Things Considered*

"For all their humor, his poems achieve an achingly familiar pathos. The melancholy we experience while reading Sirowitz perhaps stems from a shock of recognition—a feeling that part of our own life has been glimpsed. In this way, the pathetic is used as a means of telling us, humorously, sadly of our own stubborness. Through it all, his plain clothes honesty attains a pleasurable seriousness."
—Tom Devaney, Cover magazine

"These poems [in *Mother Said*] map the tangled terrain . . . of the American family—its complex relationships, its twisted fears, its desperate dreams. They're short and concise, but they can be sad, disturbing, and funny all at once: the emotional debris of an entire dysfunctional life packed into each one."
—*Details*

"[Hal]'s telling you stuff that's devastatingly sad and weird, and some of it is just hilarious, of course. For that reason, he's very black. . . . I guess I must have written 'I Palindrome I' after I saw Hal."
—John Flansburgh of They Might Be Giants, on NPR's *Studio 360*

"Hal Sirowitz blurts unspeakable truths. Horrifying, funny, and nothing you want your mother to catch you reading. Bring home a copy today!"
—A. M. Homes

"When they make a movie of his life, Jeff Goldblum will be the obvious candidate to fill the tall awkward leading role. With the syrupy voice of a Joey Ramone and a nervous, but not self-hating Woody Allen mentality, Sirowitz eminates a positive aura...."
  —Evan Dashevsky, *Hybrid Magazine*

"His deadpan humor is Jewish, tender, self-mocking and yet infused with strong feeling.... The naivete animating *Mother Said* succeeds because it is so clearly genuine and not sentimental or willed."
  —David Lehman, *The Last Avant-Garde*

"Hal Sirowitz's poems are indelible because they're incredibly funny, totally genuine, and because they're rooted in a complicated sympathy for the ambitious American family. This book will make you laugh out loud at the truth."
  —Rick Moody

"Mr. Sirowitz has a style on the page . . . of the young Philip Roth."
  —*New York Times*

"A self-styled mama's boy."
  —Bruce Weber, *New York Times*

"In Norway, Sirowitz's mother-obsessed poetry has been called 'the lyrical answer to Jerry Seinfeld.'"
  —Andrea Sachs, *Time*

"Sirowitz's poems might be the channeled voice of Philip Roth in a state of catatonic dementia."
  —*Village Voice*

Before, During & After

Poems by Hal Sirowitz

Designed by Nick Stone

Soft Skull Press
71 Bond Street
Brooklyn, NY 11217
www.softskull.com

Printed in Canada

Acknowledgements:
I'd like to thank the editors of the following magazines for publishing some of these poems: *Explosive Magazine, Hanging Loose, RealPoetik, Searching for Daylight* & *The Ledge.* I'd also like to thank the Corporation of Yaddo for giving me the time to write many of these poems. The book is dedicated to my wife, Minter Krotzer, who in no shape or form resembles any of the women portrayed in this book.

Library of Congress Cataloging-in-Publication Data

Sirowitz, Hal.
   Before, during, and after : poems / by Hal Sirowitz.—1st ed.
      p. cm.
   ISBN 1-887128-93-X (pbk. : alk. paper)
   1. Erotic poetry, American. 2. Sex customs—Poetry. I. Title.
PS3569.I725 B44 2003
811'.54—dc21

                              2003013843

Before, During & After

Taking the Sex Out

I'd stay inside my room & play
the Rolling Stones' "I Can't Get
No Satisfaction" to help me deal
with my sexual frustrations. Mother
would stick her head inside the room
& say satisfaction can also be attained
by helping her clean the house. She
kept trying to take the sex out of rock & roll.
I kept trying to put it back in. When
I went out with Jane I brought the longest song
I had, "Inna Gadda Da Vida," so we wouldn't
have to stop making out to change the record.
She said the music wasn't putting her in the mood
for sex, just for drugs. We went outside,
so she could score. She didn't invite me back in.

Before Sex

Taking the Grammar Out of the Kiss

> "A kiss can be a comma, a question mark or
> an exclamation point. That's basic spelling
> that every woman ought to know."
> —Mistinguett in *Theatre Arts*

Your kiss was like a question mark,
she said, & my lips were giving you
the answer. That was why I got mad
when you pulled away. I needed
to kiss you again to get a reprise.

On the Agenda

You're welcome to come up
& see my apartment, she said,
as long as you know that sex
won't be the first item on the agenda.
If we make love you'd have
to sleep over, so we can have
breakfast together. I already
have condoms. I'll need you to get the eggs.

The Two-Week Metamorphosis

I noticed you at this bar
two weeks ago, she said.
I was hoping you'd talk
to me, but you must prefer sluts.
Every woman I saw you with
looked like one. Now that you've
decided to talk with a respectably dressed woman
I just want to make sure you're aware of the difference.

Tom, Dick & Harry

Before we get any deeper
into this relationship, she said,
I want to say I have a large
appetite for sex. Yet, that doesn't
mean I'd have sex with any old Tom,
Dick, or Harry. I feel free to use
that expression since your name
is different. If you were Tom or Harry
I'd have avoided saying it. If you were
a Dick I wouldn't be here
with you now, because I refuse
to go out with anyone who has that name.

Disqualification

I'm glad you've never been married,
she said, because that'd have disqualified
you from going out with me. I've
been married two times. By right,
I should disqualify myself. But
I won't, since neither of my marriages
meant much. They were almost
over as soon as they started.

The Advantage of Being a Brother

I've had lots of lovers, she said,
but I've never had a brother. I
think you'd be better in that role.
The only drawback—not being able
to have sex—can be used
to our advantage, we'll stay together forever.

Where You Can't Look

I'd like to take off my pants
to show you my tattoo, she said,
but it'd be better if I waited
until our next date, so you'll
have something to look forward to.

Different Proportions

If you like my ass now, she said,
you should have seen it when I
was sixteen. It was voted the best ass
in an unofficial poll conducted at my school.
That was quite a distinction since there was
a large student body. When I gained weight
my ass got bigger. But by gaining bulk
it no longer had the same proportions.
It stands out a little too far. I thought
I'd lose weight & get the old one back
but the difficulty of following the diet
made me question the value of having
a perfect ass. Guys would think I also had
to be perfect. They'd end up becoming disappointed.

Collecting Phone Numbers

How come you never called?
she said. I gave you my phone number
when we met. Are you collecting them
like they're postage stamps that'd be
worth more the longer you held on to them?
If you are, you're in for a big surprise.
My number has already changed.

Fun, Fun, Fun When the Guy Goes Away

That's a strange question to ask
a woman at a bar, she said. "Are
you having fun?" If I wanted
to have fun I wouldn't have come here.
This is a lot of work. I have
to decide which guy, out of
all the jerks here, has the potential
of becoming my future husband.
I mostly just have looks to go on,
since the conversation is usually
minimal—like the one we're having now.

Believing in Fate

I don't have a telephone, she said,
so I can't give you a number.
I'm not a great fan of planned dates.
But if I happen to bump into you
on the street I'd be willing to go for coffee.
Let's leave it to chance. It brought
us together once. It could work a second time.
You could help fate along by hanging out
in Chelsea. That's where I live. If I
gave you any more information I'd be cheating.

The Wind Throws Back

I lied when I told you I didn't have
a phone number, she said. I wasn't
sure about you, but now that I know
you're sane & responsible—aren't you?—
I'm going to throw caution to the wind
& hope it doesn't blow back in my face.
But if you ever spent any time in a mental hospital
I'd like to know. I won't let
it prejudice me against you.
I'm willing to give you a chance,
provided you get a letter from a psychiatrist
stating your case was closed.

Not My Type

I want to steer the conversation
away from what usually happens,
she said, when two people meet—
the giving out of misleading information
for the purpose of impressing the other—
& get straight to the heart of the matter.
You're not my type. If you can convince me
that's not true I'll stand corrected. But
before you start I want you to know
that even if you succeed I can't
guarantee I'd go out with you.

People Are Strange

I've met a lot of strange types here,
she said. I wish they were required
to wear name tags saying, "Hello.
I'm strange. Talking to me can be
dangerous to your mental health."
That way I wouldn't have to waste
my time wondering if every guy
I meet is sane or not. I'd know from the start.

Showing Her My Trust

Let me say right off the bat,
she said, I never invite the guy
back to my apartment unless
I can trust him. I don't know
how long that can take. With
some guys it only takes a few dates.
Others have never gotten
to that point, like the one who's
going to meet me for dessert,
after you & I finish eating.

The Easy Part

So far this date is going well,
she said. Dinner is always
the easiest part. It's what
comes after that's the problem.
Just because a guy buys dinner
doesn't mean he deserves to have sex.
He has to do other things to show
he's worthy. In the old days
he had to slay a dragon. Nowadays
you're lucky if he helps you kill
some mice. The last guy I knew
wouldn't even pick up the traps
when he was at my house.
He told me to call an exterminator.

Checking Off the List

Before we make another date,
she said, let me tell you
the things I like to do.
Even though sex is near
the top of my list I won't
do it unless we first do
the other stuff. If you're only out
for sex I suggest you stop seeing me.
You may not want to wait until
we get to the end of the list.

Seen You Around

Each time I've come to this bar,
she said, I've seen you here.
You look like you come here often.
You must be having trouble finding
a steady girlfriend. I hope you
don't think I'm being critical.
I can't find a partner either.
I go to different bars, so it isn't as obvious.

With My Picture Underneath

When I asked you for paper,
she said, so I could write down
my phone number I can't believe
you handed me a sheet with another
woman's number on it. Should I draw
my picture underneath, & make a map
to my house, so you won't call her instead of me?

When a Date Is Not a Date

Another guy took me on a date
to this same restaurant, she said.
We didn't hit it off, but it wasn't
the food's fault. It was his fault.
He insisted I pay half the bill.
I said I thought we were on a date.
He said it was a rehearsal for a date.
I told him he should have told me that
before he had asked me out, not spring
it on me with the wine.

The Decoy

My last boyfriend is at the bar,
she said. Move closer to me,
so he'll think we're an item.
Though hey—he's not looking anymore,
so you can step back. Thanks
for doing me that favor. I'll
do the same for you. But
right now I have to go ask him something.

The Danger of Seeing Each Other Less

My last boyfriend thought we'd
have fewer problems, she said,
if we saw each other less. It worked.
It made me forget we were still a couple.
He must have forgotten too, because
he found another girlfriend.

Making It through Another Night

My favorite song, she said, is
"Help Me Make It through
the Night" by Kris Kristofferson.
I'm not interested in looking
for a relationship. I've already
been married. I've seen how
they don't work. You don't
have to worry about my asking
you to help me make it through
this night. I only like guys
who look like Kristofferson.

Absent Lovers

I'm sorry I wasn't home, she said,
even though I told you I would be.
I could tell by your message
how disappointed you were.
But I don't know why we have
to keep seeing each other
all the time. We seem to
do much better on the phone.

Deciding on the Day

I can't see you next weekend,
she said. I'll be out of town.
I doubt I'll be available that following
weekend either. In fact,
I don't see a weekend
in which I'm not tied up. I can only
see you on a weekday.
If you think that means you
can have a weekend relationship
with someone else while you're
seeing me during the week
you're mistaken. I won't stand for it.
I'd appreciate you telling me
your decision as soon as possible
because I have another guy
who's pretty quick.

Betrayed by Your Feet

Since you seem like a strong individual,
she said, I'm going to tell you the truth—
we could never be a couple. It's
not anything you said that made me
come to this conclusion. I'm basing
it solely on the position of your feet.
Your right foot is pointed away from me.
You look like you're ready to make
your escape. I need a guy who's more decisive.

The Revenge Fantasy

Whenever I give out my phone number
at a bar, she said, I always ask
the guy for his. That way if he
doesn't call I can call him & say,
"Is this the lying son of a bitch
who said he'd call? What happened?
Did you suddenly discover you
already had a girlfriend & couldn't
handle one more? Or did you sense
I'm not like the women you usually
meet? I don't take any shit."

My Friend the Secretary

I never give out my phone number
to men, she said. I give them
the number of a friend who
has my schedule, so she can
set up the date. Make sure
you tell her you're calling
in reference to me, or she'll
think you want to take her out.
That's why she does it for me.
She met a few men that way.
If the guy is that untrustworthy
she has my permission to steal him.

Guy Types

Excuse me while I put another stick
of gum in my mouth, she said.
I used to be a cigarette smoker.
I quit smoking, because I realized
the cigarettes were causing me
to go out with the same type of guy –
someone who always smokes. I
figured if I gave up smoking
not only would my lungs feel
better, but I'd meet a different type
of guy. So far I've been meeting
lots of guys who chew gum.
As a group they're not that much
better. Instead of being addicted
to nicotine they're hooked on sugar.
I may have to give up gum too if I want
to meet someone without an addiction.

We Try Harder

While I was getting a drink at the bar
a half hour ago I saw you deciding,
she said, whether you should talk to me.
I tried making your decision easier
by smiling at you, but you started
talking to someone else. I'm
your second choice. Just like
Avis has to try harder than Hertz,
I have to try to outshine the other woman.
Knowing you picked her over me
makes me want to tell you
to just go back to square one.

No Relationships Allowed

I overheard you talking to another woman
at this bar two weeks ago, she said.
You were telling her you were looking
for a relationship. That word isn't
appreciated here. You're not supposed
to put all your cards on the table.
Try using the word "fling" next time.
It may not be what you want, but it gets you more.

Down by the Sea

When I was young I thought the condoms
I found on the beach, she said, were
dead jellyfish. When I brought them home
my mother took one look at them
& threw them out. I wasn't allowed
to go to the ocean by myself anymore.
She was afraid of what it could show me.

What Fine Wisdom Teeth You Have

I know you've been disappointed
that I haven't let you show me
your penis, she said, but
there are other parts of you
I'd like to get to know first,
like your wisdom teeth. I
love your mouth. I know
from experience that once
I see your penis you won't
want me to look at anything else.

Too Big for the Closet

I live with my ex-boyfriend, she said,
but it's not what you think. He's
like a toy I've outgrown
& stuck in the closet. I couldn't
just get rid of him. He has too many
problems. I'll make sure when you
come over he stays in his room.

Round & Round the Circle We Go

Our not having slept together,
she said, may be a problem
for you, but is a godsend for me.
For once I don't feel like
I have to rush into a relationship,
but can spend time circling
around it, like an airplane
waiting to land.

Celibacy

I'm practicing being celibate again,
she said. It was hard to do while
I had a boyfriend. But now that
I no longer have one, I'm going
to take my time finding another one.
Celibacy isn't as bad as it's made out
to be. In fact, it makes me appreciate
the nuns I had in high school. I used to feel
sorry for them. I thought they were
missing out on a lot of fun, but
now I'm tired of guys pressuring me
to sleep with them. They claim
sex helps me to understand them.
But the only thing it helps me
to understand is how horny they are.

First Viewing

I haven't seen your penis yet,
she said, but I've touched it,
so I was hoping that'd count
as the same thing. My lack of curiosity
doesn't mean I'm not fond of you.
I just know that once I see it
our relationship will change.
Your penis will become the center
of attention. Right now I'd
rather it stayed on the periphery.

During Sex

Breaking My Concentration

I'm glad you're concerned about whether
I had an orgasm or not, she said, but I'd
prefer if you could wait until I was
finished before asking me about it.
It's very disconcerting, especially when
I'm on the verge of having one, for you to ask,
"Does that count as one or two?" It doesn't
count as anything if you interfere with my concentration.

Southwest of Where You Are

Let me start off by showing you
the location of my clitoris, she said,
so you'll be able to find it
by yourself. You always tend
to be somewhat southwest
of it. I don't want to have to keep
saying, "Head north. Now
go east without going further,"
as if we were taking a nice trip
in a car & not in bed.

What Men Want

They say a dog
is man's best friend,
she said, but I say
it's his penis. I've
seen men leave their
dogs alone for a day,
but they never stop
thinking about their penises
for less than a few minutes.
You may think I sound
prejudiced against men,
but it's only because
I've learned to love them
so goddamned much
that I know so much about them.

To Be Used As Directed

I'm worried now that you've
told me sex helps you fall asleep,
she said, you're going to use it
as a sleeping pill. Every time
we make love I'm going to think,
Is he doing this out of love
or just to put himself to sleep?
I'd like you to stay up for a while
to prove to me you didn't
just make love as an exercise in morphology.

Conquerors Put Their Names on Everything

It had to be a man who coined the term
"miniature penis" to describe the clitoris,
she said. Men are always naming things
after themselves. Why don't they
just call it what it is instead of trying
to make it sound like it's a much smaller
version of theirs? How would you
like it if I referred to your penis
as an oversized clitoris? You'd probably
accuse me of trying to diminish your campaign.

Back on the Farm

I grew up on a farm, she said.
I used to get up early to milk the cows.
When you squeeze my breasts
you remind me of that time.
But instead of it being a pleasant memory
you make me feel like I'm the cow.

Staying on Top

Before we start making love,
she said, let's agree that whoever
begins on top gets to stay there.
Once I'm on top I'd prefer
not to give up my position.

Not in the Mood

If you weren't in the mood
for sex, she said, you should
have told me. Instead, you
let your penis tell me. It was
a surprise when it said no.

Sliding in the Pie

Women need more time than men
to get ready for sex, she said.
You can't just turn on the oven
& slide in a pie. You have
to preheat it first by fidgeting
with the temperature control
to make sure it's as hot as it says it is.

Growling

If a dog only growls at strangers,
she said, how come you're growling
at me now. I thought the night
we took off our clothes
we became more than friends.
If you don't feel the same way
you should tell me.
I'll put my clothes back on.

Why Can't You Be Like My Dog?

The last time we made love,
she said, I put my arm
around you but your bones didn't
feel right. Your neck had become
hairy. When I opened my eyes
I saw I was hugging my dog. He
doesn't have your intellect, but he knows
better than to stop being affectionate
after he gets what he wants.

Beginning with a Kiss

I don't usually sleep with the guy
on the first date, she said. That's
why I'm surprised we slept together tonight.
I didn't think kissing you would be
so dangerous. I've kissed plenty
of guys without them ending up
in my bed. But it wasn't how you
kissed me that did it. It was
the way you held me. I wanted
to hold you too, but the only thing
I was in position to hold was your penis.

Muffling the Sound

I didn't want to take any of your enjoyment
away, she said, while you were having
an orgasm, by asking you to keep
the noise down, but it was making me
nervous. If my landlord can hear
the toilet flush, then she definitely
heard you. I wouldn't be surprised
if she puts her ear against the wall
to hear you better. Next time
try putting your hand over our mouths.

The Difference between the Sex Organs

Kissing is the gateway to sex,
she said. Groping my breasts
or putting your hand between
my legs does nothing for me
unless you start off with kissing.
Sometimes you act as if there's
no difference between our sex organs.
Yours doesn't take much time
to get ready, but mine needs help.
It doesn't operate on automatic.

Excavation

I keep telling you it's not
my vagina that causes
the pleasurable sensations,
she said. It's my clitoris.
Yet you persist in wasting time
down there, like an archaeologist
trying to find remnants
of a lost civilization,
digging at the wrong site.

Some Things You Can't Recycle

You're not supposed to reuse
the condom, she said, if you
put it on wrong. You're
supposed to throw it out.
It may have gotten damaged.
I know it's a waste of a good condom,
but it's not like I'm going to report you
to the Green Party or some other
ecological group. I don't think
they care about those things.
You just have to swallow some stuff,
like your ecological pride, & make sure
you get it on properly.

The Person in the Next Seat

You can't just sneak up on my sex organs,
she said, & expect me to become aroused.
You have to work your way
to them. You should see it as embarking
on a long trip. Half the fun is the stops along the way.

"This" over "That"

I'm glad you stopped
touching me like "that," she said,
& are now touching me like "this."
There's a big difference between
a "this" & a "that." A "that"
makes me feel like the railing
on a staircase. You're holding on
to me so you won't slip. But
it's the "this" that gives me pleasure.

Tall Tale

Make sure you flush the condom
down the toilet, she said. You
don't have to worry about an alligator
eating it & choking to death. There
aren't any alligators living in the sewers.
It's just an urban legend. Your father
probably told you that, because he
didn't want you spending too much time
on the toilet. He probably needed to sit there.

Not Needing It Now

The next time you hand me a condom
to throw away, she said, kindly
make sure it's right side up, so
the contents won't spill.
One day I may need your sperm
to produce a child, but until
that day I'd rather not have it on me.

With the Water Pouring Down

I just put on new sheets,
she said, so I thought we
could make love in the shower instead.
We wouldn't have to worry
about getting anything dirty.
But I'm not so sure how comfortable
it'd be. It might take the enjoyment
out of sex. Then I'd have to get
my enjoyment some other way—
like having a conversation—
but I wouldn't want to put you through that.

That Tingling Feeling

That orgasm was good, she said.
It shook me out of my stupor.
I can still feel my skin tingling.
I'm sorry you didn't have one too,
though it wasn't my fault. You
waited too long. I'll let you share
some of the pleasure I got from mine.
I'm going to be nice to you all day.
I won't act moody. Hopefully,
you'll notice the difference.

Full Cycle

I'd love to rub chocolate syrup
over your body, she said, then
slowly lick it off. Unfortunately,
it's too fattening. When I put on
some extra pounds I stop feeling
good about myself. I don't like
to be seen naked when I get like that.
If I'm not naked, how are we supposed
to have sex? It's a vicious cycle.
It's easier to just do it without the chocolate.

Experiments

I'd love to experiment sexually,
she said, & buy a Far Eastern sex manual,
like the *Kama Sutra*, but I'm hesitant
about starting something new
when I don't know how long
this relationship will last.
I don't do any experiments
unless I know I can finish them.

Getting the Scream to Blend In

I don't mind you always being
on top when we make love, she said,
as long as you let me be the DJ—
I can't make love to Frank Sinatra.
He reminds me too much of my parents.
I need louder music, like the Sex Pistols,
so if I have an orgasm & let out
a scream it'll blend right in, & not
sound like I'm hitting a wrong note.

The Act of Floating

After I have an orgasm, she said,
I feel like I'm floating. It's like
I'm no longer physically on this bed.
I'm far away—above the clouds,
somewhere in the stratosphere.
But I don't stay there for long.
Inevitably, you're always scratching
some part of your body, breaking
the spell, & bringing me back
to earth. I just wish you'd do
all your scratching before we begin.

How Dogs Let Each Other Know

A female dog has to lift up
one of her back legs, she said,
to let the male know she wants
to have sex. I don't even have
to do that. I only have to bend
my knee & you pounce on me.
You never let sex be my idea.

The Meaning of Sex

The fact that I've picked you out
of all the men who wanted
to sleep with me, she said,
should make you feel special.
I need to feel special too.
It was a close contest.
I shouldn't tell you this, but I'm
still in touch with the runner-up.

The Crime of Staying Indoors

You wouldn't guess from looking
at you, she said, you'd have so much
sexual energy. When we get into bed
you become like Superman, but instead
of putting on a costume you
stay naked. I should get
you a cape, so you can put it on
& stop the real crime—not getting out
of bed on such a beautiful day.

Standard Model

I've always been self-conscious
about my body, she said, so
the less you stare at my vagina
the more comfortable I'll be.
I know you've seen one before.
Mine can't be that different.
It's not like the kitchen faucet
that comes in many models.
It's pretty standard. Just remember
I haven't used it in a while.
You may have to spend time
getting it back in working order.

My Father the Gynecologist

My father is my gynecologist, she said.
My girlfriends wonder how I can use him.
Doesn't it feel strange, they say, having
your father examine your most private part.
It does feel a little odd when I first take off
my panties but he's very quick about it.
Sometimes he does both my mother & me.
The best part is he doesn't charge. Once
I tried going to a stranger. I had to wait
in her office a long time. She wasn't
as good as him, but was expensive.
The main drawback is he knows too much
about my sex life. When I brought boyfriends
over to their house he never acted friendly.
Maybe it was because he knew how many
urinary tract infections I had gotten from each one.
When whatever boyfriend was living with me
would answer the phone my father would remind him
to wash his hands. That boyfriend would get annoyed.
I've stopped taking my boyfriends home.
I hope you don't feel left out if you don't meet
my parents. My father already knows about you.
I had to tell him some of your medical history.
He hasn't said anything critical about you yet.

Since we've been sleeping together I haven't
gotten one infection. Let's hope our good luck continues.

The Name Game

She decided to give my penis
a name. I don't know why
she gave it a Spanish one.
She said it looked Spanish.
How could it have a different
nationality than me? But
when she spoke Spanish
she'd get more excited
& touch it more. So I
didn't say anything, but
as soon as I got home it
became American again.

After Sex

The Decline of Kissing

I've noticed that the amount of times
you've been kissing me, she said,
has been declining at a steady rate
the more we have sex. I'm hoping
it doesn't stop altogether. Sex
without kissing is like a gift you forgot to wrap.

Hammer in Hand

While I studied Personal Hygiene
& Sexuality in high school, she said,
you were taking Shop—learning how to bang
in a nail. You're good at hammering
away at something, but when
our relationship breaks down
I'm the one who knows how to fix it.

Less Is More

The problem with having sex now, she said,
is we won't have anything to do later.
We can't just sleep with each other every time
we have nothing to do. Repetition
cheapens it. That's why in the old days
couples used to wait to get married
before they had sex. They wanted
something to look forward to. I'm
not advocating that we stop having sex,
only that we wait a little longer before
doing it again. I want to savor
the experience. You only want to repeat it.

Making It Public

Doesn't the fact that we made love,
she said, mean we're now a couple?
Can we hold hands in public?
Or are you still not ready to announce it?
The quicker we tell others the more chance
it has of becoming true. I'm not
even sure I believe it. I hope you
don't wait so long that by the time
you acknowledge me, we're no longer
a couple. I'd hate to have to use
the past tense when talking about us.

Bedroom Traffic

You helped me break my most important
rule—never sleep with anyone
on the first date—so how come,
she said, you're so concerned
about my breaking a simple traffic rule?
If you're so uptight about my making
an illegal U-turn, then you should
have waited longer before sleeping with me,
so you could have seen how I drive.

Conversion of Energy

Instead of kissing & hugging me
when I get home, she said, which
you don't need to do since you're
already in a permanent state of arousal,
you should try converting
your sexual energy into something
less potent—like using it to water the plants.
When I'm adjusted to being back home,
then you can turn the energy back
to its original form, because I'd have time to get ready.

Favoring the Nose

The fact that you had to hide your penis
from other men, she said whenever you
used the lockers or bathrooms
makes you want to show it
to me more. But I'd
rather look at your nose.
At least when something comes out
of it you cover it up
with a handkerchief. You don't get it all over me.

Making It into a Nocturnal Activity

It's already too late to go to the museum,
she said. I knew we shouldn't have
had sex, but once your hormones
kick in there's no stopping you.
I don't know when we'd have
another chance to see that exhibit.
You have to train your libido
to become more nocturnal.
That's when everyone else has sex,
so it won't interfere with the day's
activities. So repeat after me,
"No sex before or immediately
after dinner." We should only
do it after we've put away the dishes.

You're Nothing but a Hound Dog

I could do with less sex, she said,
& more kissing & hugging. But if
they're only done for the purpose
of having sex I'd leave them out too.
The risk I'd be taking is you might get bored,
& either leave me or start to look like
a hound dog, with your tongue out.
But don't expect me to sleep with you
to get you to put your tongue back.
You'd have to put it back yourself.

Flat Bread

I'm convinced you gave me my yeast infection,
she said. I don't eat wheat, so I couldn't
have given it to myself. The last time
we had sex you had just finished eating
a sandwich. The yeast must have come
from that bread. Yeast makes bread rise,
so the flatter the bread the less yeast
inside. Next time try eating a flatter
bread. Or you could try washing
your hands more, but you'll have
to be careful about which soap
you use. I'm sensitive to that, too.

Directness

Did any of your former girlfriends
ever tell you, she said, that you
have sex on the brain? That's
all you think about. I'm sure
they weren't as frank as me.
Instead of telling you,
they just stopped seeing you.

Letting It Sleep

You must have heard the expression
"Let sleeping dogs lie," she said,
so let's not wake up your penis.
Let it stay asleep. It's probably
dreaming about my vagina, so it's not
like you're depriving it of anything.

Not a Cause of Death

No one died from lack of sex,
she said. So you're not going
to die if I don't sleep with you
tonight. I know I said I would,
but I said that when I was in
a different mood. I'm not
always in control of my moods,
just like you're not in control
of when you can do it.

Penis in a Jar

If you have a need for women
to see your penis, she said,
you should donate it to science.
It'll be preserved in a bottle
of formaldehyde. Female
medical students will wonder what
it did to merit such attention.
Luckily for you I don't intend
to be there to tell them the truth.
It was mainly used to bother me.

I'll Make You Stay

I want to show you my winter clothes,
she said. Since we've only known
each other this summer you've never
seen any of these dresses on me.
Don't you like this one with the
strapless back? All this is in store
for you if we stay together.

Red, Red Bra

I bought a red bra, she said.
I knew you'd like it.
The only problem was I didn't
have a red blouse to wear with it.
I bought that & red pants
& shoes, so it wouldn't stand out
so much. I also thought of getting
red panties. But I said to hell with that.
I'm not going to worry if one small part
of the outfit doesn't match. And who's
going to see my underwear? Just you.
What do you know about fashion? Nothing.

Extending the Life of Clothes

In the interest of saving my bras
from the wear & tear of your hands,
she said, I've decided to go without
one today. But that doesn't mean
I'm advocating having sex.
I've slept with men since
I was a teenager, & in that time
I've learned a few things, like
I have to take my bra off
from time to time if I want it to last.

G-string

Just imagining you in the women's section
trying to find underwear in my size,
she said, was worth more
than what you had to pay for them.
It gave me a good laugh. The underwear
didn't amuse me in the same way.
In fact, they got me thinking, Does
he think of me as a whore? That's
generally who buys this kind of panties.
I'd never buy them for myself.
They have no support for my rear end.
It's too big to be held up by a string.

Sexy Underwear

I know you like buying me underwear,
she said, but what am I going to do
if people at my job keep asking
whether you bought me anything yet—
drop my pants & give them a look?

R-E-S-P-E-C-T

You show a lot of self-control
when it comes to food, she said.
I've seen you eat half a slice of cake,
then save the rest for later. But
I've never seen you caress my top half,
then save the bottom half for another time.
The moment you touch the top I can tell
you have designs on the bottom. I
want you to treat my body with the same respect
you show food. You shouldn't be
gobbling it all up in one sitting.

The Act of Counting

It's a sign of obsessive-compulsive behavior,
she said, to count how many times
we made love. I've never counted.
Even if we stopped having sex for a while
we'd still be way ahead of where we ought to be
in terms of times a couple usually has sex.
It's the most I've done it.
It tops every other relationship. But if
we stopped for too long you'd probably
end the relationship, because you'd
have one less thing to count. I wouldn't want
you to replace it by counting the days until you leave.

The Road to Her Heart

The way to a woman's heart
is not through sex, she said.
That's only a detour. You've got
to get back on the main road.
I'm not going to tell you where
that is. You have to find it yourself.
Try bringing her flowers, & involving
her in your life. There's no
guarantee you'll get there,
but at least you're heading in the right direction.

My Side of the Bed

I don't mind getting you aroused,
she said, as long as you stay
on your side of the bed. But
once you come on mine
you can't expect me to stop
whatever I'm doing, like reading
a book, to relieve you of your condition.
First, I'd want to make sure I was
the cause of it, that it wasn't
the result of your thinking about
old girlfriends. Then I'd like
you to check & see what mood
I was in. Keep that in consideration.

Not to Cease from Our Exploration

You're making our relationship
one-dimensional, she said.
It's starting to resemble
a porno picture. I'd like it
to be more inclusive. There
are other things to explore
besides each other's bodies.
It'd just be nicer if we traveled
some place for real.

The Impossible Dream

The fact that you brought a dozen condoms
for our trip this weekend, she said,
either means you're bad at math
or you're just unrealistic. It'll be
almost impossible to sleep with you
that many times in that time span.
If we did achieve that feat we wouldn't
have time to do anything else. There'd
be no point in our having gone away
if we had to spend all our time inside.

Getting Rid of His Ghost

I didn't sleep well last night,
she said. The bed felt crowded,
even though you didn't take up
too much space. I realized
I still miss my last boyfriend.
It was like his ghost was still
in the bed. That was why
I woke you up to have sex.
It's my only way of driving him away.

Later

Take Him, He's Yours

If I see you staring again
at another woman, she said,
I'm going to escort you
to her table, make the introductions,
& say, "You can have him.
I don't want him anymore."
I'd let her know what
your résumé in relationships
looks like—too many girlfriends
& a shortage of commitment.
I'd tell her about us—
the last relationship on your list.
She won't want you either.

Wedged

You were the one who followed me
into the elevator & asked
for my phone number, she said.
I didn't lead you on. In fact,
I tried discouraging you.
I told you I had lots of problems.
I was used to being alone. But now
that you've wedged yourself into my life,
don't think leaving me will be as smooth
as our first elevator ride. It'll be
like walking up a flight of stairs.

Thirty Days of Hell

All you do is show up, she said.
Lately, you haven't even done that.
Last night you claimed you had
important things to take care of
& needed to be somewhere else.
If you're thinking of not seeing me
anymore I want advance notice, preferably thirty days.

The Blouse that Didn't Stay On

I was annoyed at the film's director,
she said, for having the actress
take off her blouse in two scenes.
I already saw her breasts. Nothing
about them had changed.
I didn't even want to see them
the first time. I didn't appreciate
how you almost stood in your seat,
so you could see better. You
were showing me disrespect.
If the actor had taken off
his pants & exposed his genitals
I wouldn't have leaned over
to get a better view.

Sex & Marriage Go Together

You keep saying I should consider
this vacation as our honeymoon,
she said, but that's what you said
on our last vacation. How many
honeymoons can we have? I
want to get married only so I
can have a real one & not be
bothered with all these fakes.

Putting Off My Good-bye

The reason I slept with you last time,
she said, was because I didn't
feel like saying good-bye. I
wanted to put it off until the morning.
But now I have even more trouble saying it,
because I can tell you're in love with me.
I want to feel free to say it anytime I want,
without having to worry about hurting you.

The Next Block

I hope you're not trying to make
our relationship into a long-distance one,
she said. That's what my last boyfriend
did. He liked the idea of not seeing
me as much, even though he lived
on the next block. At least
you live further away.

Only with a Camera Does It Count

What's the point of going on a trip,
she said, if you forgot to bring
the camera? We have no way
of documenting it. It's like we
never went. The purpose of
going away is to bring back
pictures, so I can show people
you took me somewhere. Now
they'll have to take my word for it.
That's not as convincing as pictures.

When Your Hand Is Your True Lover

Even if our relationship didn't
work out, she said, at least you
got something from it—a nice
long break from masturbating.

The Missing Ring

If you intend to marry me,
she said, shouldn't you
have gotten me an engagement ring?
All my friends say, "Did
he get you one yet?"
I tell them he's working on it.
They say he doesn't have
to make one. He only has to buy it.

The Trip to Somewhere

Promising me you're going to take me
on a trip, she said, is not the same
as taking me on one. There's
a big difference between a promise
& reality. The trip might never happen.
I don't care where we go as long as it's somewhere.
I want to get it over with,
so I can see what your next promise will be.

When There's No Message

I can't understand how you can
accuse me of never listening to you,
she said. Haven't I always asked
for your opinion? If you didn't
give one I had no choice but to use
my own. They say you can't blame
the messenger for the message.
But if there's no message, then you'd
have to blame the person who didn't
give the messenger the message. That'd be you.

Peeking Inside the Drawer

This is where I keep my underwear,
she said. You can take a quick peek,
& see what's in store for you the longer
you go out with me. The more
relaxed I am around you the skimpier
the underwear I'll wear. After a while
I won't have to wear any. You'd like that,
wouldn't you? Though, I wouldn't
want to do that on a regular basis.
They cost too much not to wear.

Running in Place

I've been married already, she said.
I told myself I'd never do it again.
But if we didn't get married, people
would think our relationship went nowhere.
Even if we got divorced it's still not
as big a failure as if we never married.
Divorce may not be the most pleasant
experience, but at least you get papers
to remember it by. Whereas, if we
live together & break up it's like it never happened.

Rattlesnakes

Men are always undressing me in their minds,
she said. I don't have to be a scientist
to figure that out. The evidence is
in their eyes. I don't want you to think
I have anything against men. I don't.
I have nothing against rattlesnakes either,
but since I've never seen one outside
the zoo, I don't have to worry about them much.
Men are harder to avoid. Since you seem
to be different from the typical man
I'm letting my guard down. But if I
find you're just putting on an act,
& deep down you're just like them,
don't be surprised if you hear me scream herpetology.

Little Bee

If a little bee can hurt me,
she said, just think of what
you're capable of doing.
You're a thousand times bigger.
I should be more scared of you.
The bee is only mad at me
if I get in its way, which
doesn't happen much. But
if I decide not to sleep with you
you act like I'm denying you
a basic human right. If we have sex
you become harmless, but if I decide not to,
then I have to be on the lookout for your sting.

When the Kissing Stopped

She said she preferred kissing
over sex. She wanted to do more
of that & less of the other.
Then one day she refused to do
either. She said she was fed up
with my not kissing her enough.
I was only interested in sex.
I thought I could do both
at the same time. I didn't realize
she needed to keep them separate.

Counting the Times

I've long since lost count, she said,
of how many times we made love.
Maybe when we first started having sex
I could give you a close estimate,
but now I have no idea. It must
be some ridiculously large number.
But to a person like you, nothing
can ever be too much. You always
want more, whether it's food or sex.
I don't mind you eating to your heart's content,
as long as you're not taking my portion.

The Bigger Problem

The problem we're now having,
she said, is minor compared
to the bigger problem
of why we're continuing
to stay together even if we're not
getting along. I have to remind
myself not to get into a tailspin
watching you use cold water to wash the silverware,
but should be mainly concerned
with the impending collapse.

Paris Without You

I didn't mind you promising
to love me forever, she said,
because that's what lovers are
supposed to say. But to make
a site-specific promise—
taking me to Paris—then end
our relationship before we have
a chance to go there is extremely
disturbing. You put that idea
in my head. Now I'll have to go there
by myself. When you knew you
were breaking up with me you should
have weaned me from wanting to go
to such a far away place & suggested
some place nearer. When you get
my postcard don't expect it to say,
"Wish you were here." Most likely
it'll say, "You son of a bitch.
They speak French in Montreal, too,
& it's cheaper to get there."

About the Author

Hal Sirowitz is the poet laureate of Queens, New York, and is the recipient of a Frederick Delius Award, the Susan Rose Recording Grant for Contemporary Jewish Music, a National Endowment for the Arts Fellowship, and a 2003 New York State Foundation for the Arts Fellowship. His book *Mother Said* has been translated into nine languages. Sirowitz has performed on MTV's *Spoken Word Unplugged*, PBS's *Poetry Heaven*, and NPR's *All Things Considered, Studio 360,* and the *Leonard Lopate Show,* as well as on numerous stages across the country. Sirowitz is also the bestselling translated poet in

Norway, where *Mother Said* has been adapted for the stage and has been made into a series of animated cartoons. His poems have been included in dozens of anthologies such as Garrison Keillor's *Good Poems*, Billy Collins's *Poetry 180, Poetry in Motion from Coast to Coast, Poetry after 9/11,* and *110 Stories: Writers Respond to 9/11.* Sirowitz was a special education teacher for the New York City public schools for twenty-three years. Despite what the exes in this book predicted, Hal is now happily married to the writer Minter Krotzer.